Vision of Lucha

Vision of Lucha

Marjorie Sadin

GOLDFISH PRESS

Published by
Goldfish Press, Seattle
2012 18th Ave. South
Seattle, WA 98144

Manufactured in the United States of America

ISBN 9780971160163
Library of Congress Catalog Card Number 2014948301

Contents

My goal in writing *Vision of Lucha* is to describe my struggle, lucha
meaning struggle in Spanish, to survive with a disability. My poems
come from a deeply personal autobiographical source, but they
include universal themes—love, death and family. *Vision of Lucha*
is a compilation of earlier poems with very recent ones. I have four
books of poetry in print with many poems published nationally. It
took great courage to publish the poems in *Vision of Lucha* about
my experiences and the history of mental illness in my family. I
explore other issues like God, gender and race. My vision of *Vision
of Lucha* is to reach out to my audience —whether it is through my
disability or the death of my mother. — *Marjorie Sadin*

The Violin and the Lady in Black

for David

This is their film-noir.
He—half-naked playing the violin.
She—dressed in a black evening gown.

She tries listening but falls asleep
to his tremolo, his crescendo.
He plays as if the violin were her—
and she's jealous of the other woman—
the violin—that he plays like he plays her.

In his film-noir, she is a vixen, a temptress—
like the devil in Cocteau's Orpheus—
a woman in a black evening gown.

And he wants her this way.
But she doesn't want to be
his muse, a vixen—but rather
him playing the violin as *her* muse.

And she cuts and splices her film-noir to capture
the man she is in love with.

And the finale comes when he climbs into bed with her.
She pretends to be his violin.

Coals

The moon swivels a little to left.
Father lifts wood to keep it going.
I dream of evenings reading Neruda
with you out loud, first repeating the Spanish
then the English in time to the Rite of Spring.
The fire is nearly out.

Wherever people go when they are gone
is like the flame, dwindling, flashing,
then disappearing behind some black log
that falls apart when you touch it.
If I am touching you it is only because
you are on the other side, or rather inside
that log that falls apart.

The moon hides behind clouds.
In the morning when I wake up, the curtains
are closed. When I draw them light comes
in my room like a prism.
Morning is a miracle.

Foggy Bottom

Once a marsh, Foggy Bottom bred our ancestors—
plankton, bacteria, ameba. The witches brew mixed
just the right chemicals to create life.

Now we meet at Starbucks in Foggy Bottom—
you steal the newspaper. I sip a macchiato.
We spend our weekends at the library
on different floors. No less connected knowing you're
somewhere near.

The witches are back with their brew. They mix
shaving cream, beetle juice, a book of Byron, an
old rendition of Brahms violin concerto by
Isaac Stern, underarm hair, and a bra.
And create love.

The cauldron can only be
supernatural
because when I'm with you
anything is possible.

What is Real

David is sleeping in. I'm waiting at Starbucks
and sipping my macchiato.

Weekends are ours ostensibly.
We read together at the library.

I had a friend once—
Michelle—who I called on the phone and spoke to
over the weather. When I called back the rings answered
me —one for yes, two for no, three for I love you.

It has been 18 years since I talked to Michelle over the weather.
David is real. Just this morning I warmed my hands on his
testicles and we discussed poetry.

Touching him is like touching a rose petal.
And I'll never hear from Michelle again.

Something Not So Scary

Something not so scary
as my impaled heart,
or my first day of work
in quite awhile.

After hours of separation we
become something new
like a vision.

It is not scary to us, or rather is scary
but we do it anyway—the name of a self-help
book I promised my sister I would study.

But isn't scary something I did
as a child at a campfire?
Or the way I felt when I
almost lost my mother entirely?
Is it just something that can't be avoided—
something primordial and necessary?

And if I went back to the beginning,
not of time—which would be daunting—
but to when we met and laughed
nervously, yes, that's a fear I could put up with,
gladly.

And the fear of having you and losing you
and not knowing which will happen next
gives way to a certain calm when you lie down next to me
and fear falls away like my clothes.

Leather

I am carving you
a leather watch band.
I am not sure
it is for you, I pound
flowers with a steel tool
and wooden mallet, as I might
hit your door
with my fist until it
resounds.

I work alone mostly.
Solitude puts a certain edge
on everything, including
the repetitious fantasy
of you looming over my shoulder.
You are angry that I won't
show you what I am doing.

It is my anger that presses a stem
of the wet leather
and forms a leaf almost
daintily with the tinny tap
of the mallet. These sounds
are mine ostensibly, yet my

fingers articulate their own
language.

You never see me carve
leather. It is something
I do alone, a voice
I strive to shape out of the raw
places—named emotion skewered
into words that on your palate
might not grate. This is the way
that I say to the world
that I have patience with their hate,
while you and I try to find ways
to make your anger bloom like the lips
of flowers that I shape.

Feheresad. Brooks. There is something
about the sacred moments that makes
us jubilant as crooks to find their
works. And we cannot understand how
their anger is our own. I have seen others
at work alone. You croon.
It is merely in the tone. I wrestle
with you sometimes in my sleep. We
have our own ways to keep
the world away.

The wet leather smells like hay.
I pestle in your name and write
an epigram above. Please don't
tell me that this work was done
out of anything but love.

Ode to John Berryman

In the blue light,
I am marooned,
I bearer of myself
& the world's ills.
Half of me loves and fights,
the other succumbs.
Shine your shoes, sir?
The world is definitely
a better place with me
& all my ills.

Berryman, I love you.
You saw the indecision
right through to the end.
You see me philander
for words and gods.
Teach me to unlove the way
your heavy heart headed
for the Pacific.
All your unlove and you
left the world
"a woolen lover."
Your bed is dark linen;
your sheets are silk worm.
Berryman, get up again
& sing.

Two-thirty.
The clock rings somewhere,
but not here.
Is there a God "roughhewn
and playful?" He must be
a woman for all that hot thick
breeze and maple leaves.
My throat aches;
my rage shakes.
Perhaps God is a transvestite.

My bed waits,
alone,
empty.
With all my woes,
I tell Mr. Bones
some funny story
and hold his dark hands all night.
While Berryman rolls over and talks to us
as if everything were alright.

The Cricket

Crickets murmur while supersonic noises
cut thorough the sounds of Hispanic men conversing outside.
There's something wrong. The TV blares across the hall.
Occasionally an ambulance rushes God knows where.
My mind blurs like a fast fan. Peace might arrive
if I were to dive into a lake or fall asleep. A car
skids outside. I would circle a lot that's wrong,
diminish it to silence. But sometimes I hear
the cricket's call above any other sound. They rustle through
the grass, buzz to attract each other. They recite a mantra.
I want to form few words, to persist beneath the
moonlight .When the world and my thoughts veer too near like a
targeted bomber, I only want to chirp in the grass
like a cricket rubbing his legs to be heard in the
twilight hour.

The River

The river reaches and swells. I might
have left a photograph, a silk blouse,
or something you held that night I walked
out.

The river floods and flows..
I left to bury my face in the palm
of night. You stood at the door and told
me not to go.

The night sky hushes the river. If I were
with you I might try not to walk away.
I'm not afraid of the river anymore
that sleeps cold and tired, curled up
on the shore

The Café

Where the wealthy eat pate and drink half carafes
of wine over a leisurely lunch is where I go when
I'm tired of watching soaps and sending out resumes.
I pretend I'm rich and throw in a big tip for
the waitress cleaning the table of the couple
who hardly touched their eggs benedict. I pretend
I'm wealthy as I sip espresso and bite my lip
as the ladies next door discuss their trips
to Italy and the coast of Venezuela. I come
to the café to escape the self that hates to go out.

It's like the movies. Just sit back and nibble
your popcorn. The cafes. What would I do without
them. The black market guarantee of serenity. I
sit as long as I can. It is better than the catwalk
I do in my apartment, the news at seven reiterated
at eleven. It's a crowd of hats and vests and six hundred
dollar sandals and cigarettes that sit all day
and all night and make dramatic conversation. And
by not saying a word, I fit in.

The Pawn Broker

The exigent Pawn Broker
has good deals—my father's stop watch
for a silver wine glass.

Only it is not *things* I exchange on Yom Kippur.

On Yom Kippur, I exchange the gloves of sin
for the boots of resolve.

I exchange the snap shot of selfishness
for the cameo of compassion.

The knife of betrayal
for the fork of veracity.

The hat of importance
for the necklace of modesty.

The cymbals that say too much
for the hush of the cello.

The shirt of blood
for the washed sheet of peace.

The unforgiving lamp
for the window pane's countenance.

The disbelief of the newspaper
for the trust in a map.

The wrinkled shirt of desperation
for the grace of the evening gown.

The most expensive gift
for the most expansive thought.

Lenses

Wide, blue somewhere between sunsets, I thought I knew.
Memory is easy now. The first stirrings of love in a child
I thought I knew.

But I admit to unicorns, and Pluto, the farthest from the Sun,
and feelings that widen like ripples. Because it's true
that our lenses are a little cloudy and blue is no longer blue.

The litmus test. Am I base today or acid? Pink and blue.
Will I ever know?

What I do know is like a fragmented dream I piece together
mornings. I guess my heart was asleep. I thought I knew
before I knew.

My name is fact. So is my date, sex, time of birth, age
and location. The rest is sand blown into glass that clouds
with heat and cools with time.

There is no perfect glass.

Familiar Sounds

Here in this room off the highway
where the curve of black and black
hit a buzzing VACANT sign
you lie back on a bedspread.

Propped sideways on the head-
board, you follow the chord
of the phone to its root
lifting the hollow stem that's
barely a arm's length away
to your own sore neck.

And with your thumb, you spin
back holes to their seventh number
till the bring, bring ceases
and you listen for an answer at the other
end, breath tighter than eyelids.

It clicks and you're there!
The voice torrents past but
you can hear that fine
clear breath, a buck panting
through entangled vines.

When words are gone
you're gripping the phone.

Jaylen

Jaylen dozes in class.
His little brother kicks him in bed
so he can't sleep at night.

I am his tutor. He hugs me.
I say, "not allowed." Reluctantly.

He is like a man
Taller than I am
and only 12.

Jaylen is at the 3rd Grade level,
ADD and socially mixed up.
Whatever he reads doesn't matter
Now he reads sentences instead of
sounding out letters.

And now he is teaching his younger brother
how to read letters
And he is a man to his brother.

The Potomac is Still

Snow over the ice.

I remember ice skating on the river,

unafraid that the ice might break and give way.

How do the little rivers of my dreams

bring me back to you as if we had never parted?

We skated on that river too far out—there were warnings,

the ice breaking beneath us.

Still the thrill of going out too far—

risking danger and sex.

What followed—

I drowned into your arms.

When the thaw comes,

I will be washed up ashore.

Seattle

(on the 1973 Arab-Israeli war)

Tanks rumble up hills,.
We watch Golda Meier on TV,
not understanding the Hebrew
only knowing it was time to leave.

At home, Seattle has more stars than you dreamed.
Father tells you about satellites.
Mother isn't listening; she stares
at her hands, "What's it all for? What's it
all for?"

Next day you walk through the woods
faster and faster till the tall trees
and sun come together.

You can't go home. You don't think
you'll find your way out of these woods.
Darkness settles in. You run till you find
the sun half-way through.

Mother was worried. You try
to explain. The war rumbles
far away.

Faces on a Totem Pole

Faces on a totem pole. The Sky God, the God of the Sun and the Moon. The Coyote. Papa is old. But he is sowing his oats. And Momma died. Grandma Eva died. She was old. But Grandma Rebecca and Grandpa Al died young.

Papa has a night on the town. He had his teeth fixed. He's still strong. Grandpa Ruby died in an automobile accident. I never knew him.

Totem poles. My ancestors talk to me at night sometimes. I cried when Grandma Rebecca and Grandpa Al died. Grandpa Al came to me in the eyes of an old woman. He is somewhere spirits are.

Momma had a long life, but she drank and cursed. Papa will live longer. He doesn't believe in the Spirit. I cried when Momma died, too. But then I just got scared. The Death God scared me. He with his mask so I wouldn't recognize him.

The Coyote howls. My father howls when he thinks of Momma. I can't howl back. I am still his child. My gaze shifts to the woods. There, the Wind God whispers through the trees the names of those who have died and tells where momma's ashes are scattered.

All the souls I have ever known live inside me. They bleed like ink on a page. I write about them but they write through me. When I wrote I love you to them,
I tore through the page.

Totem Poles Carved in Stone

Grandpa Ruby died in an automobile accident. Grandma Eva never remarried. I was four when Grandpa Ruby died.

Papa has his father's anger. Momma drank and tried to commit suicide. Papa said it was my responsibility to take care of Momma. I was fourteen when she tried to die.

I worship ancestors –alive and dead. Scary faces carved in stone. Totem Poles.

Grandma Eva is dead now. So are my mother's parents—Grandpa Al and Grandma Rebecca. Now Momma is dead, too. Papa is strong. He's 87. I can't imagine life without him.

Grandpa Ruby was from Russia. He married Grandma Eva when she was seventeen. I don't remember him at all. When they brought his painting in I went in the orange room and my temper flared.

Grandpa Ruby's head hit a tombstone and he died of internal bleeding. So father lost his father, and someday I will lose mine.

Totem Poles of My Dreams

Grandma Rebecca smoked Kent cigarettes. So did Grandpa Al.
I smoked Marlboro Lights.

Grandpa Al and Grandma Rebecca came to me in delusions. Grandpa Al
was Albert Einstein. Grandma Rebecca typed letters she wrote through
me. Momma has died, too. She visits me drunk or crying. I drank and
smoked just like my mom.

I thought I would live forever. Grandma Rebecca and Grandpa Al are
dead forty years now. And Momma died just last year. I gave up alcohol
and cigarettes.
The dreams persist.

Totem Poles

for Noah

Now I'm Tia, a great aunt. And Noah sleeps in my niece's arms
who breast feeds him. Someday I will be on the totem pole.
What will he remember?

He will never know my mother, or my mother's mother.
They would have wept aloud with elation.
Yet prayed to their better angels
Bacchus the god of drink their downfall.

Who will Noah take after? Hopefully not me. When I was eighteen,
they said I couldn't have a child or the child might inherit my crazy
DNA.
But I had imaginary children—Rebecca named for my grandma and
a son named Seth When I told people, they didn't believe me.

Now I'm the great aunt holding an infant in my arms light as a cup of tea.
His wide eyes tell the whole story, like my dead grandfather's eyes
in the eyes of an old woman. Taking in the world all at once, alive
and from the dead.

M grandfather was a chemistry teacher. He made green turn to red,
liquid to fire. In the blink of the eye, my mother is here
for this astonishing child.

My Sister Turns 60

My sister is a grandma now. Noah, her grandson, crawls and walks.
She lives in Wyoming, far from us. We used to scratch and bite.
She'd tease. I'd reciprocate. She taught me how to drink vodka out
of the bottle and so no one would know, replace it with water. She'd
sneak out late at night. She did acid and mescaline and made me
believe they were like fairy tails. I had bummers. She got married
young.

I wanted long straight hair like hers. Mine was curly and short.
She was blond. I was a redhead. She knew all the latest dances—
the monkey and the fruge. We danced together while listening to
American Bandstand. She was my big sister. She was popular. I was
not .

Later she told me she felt like she never had parents. That our
family was broken beyond repair. The mother I later took care of
as a child when she got drunk. My father losing his temper every
night. She and my father fight.

But everyone crowds around Noah, oohing and ahing, holding him,
and throwing him in the air and upside down. My sister makes
funny noises and talks to him as if he were an adult. Noah is the
only hope of reconciliation between my father and herself.

Them (A Sestina)

How often he thought that she forgot the time
when snowflakes melted in the breasts of sparrows.
When she was cold and shivered in the wind
and she turned to him, he called her "rainbow."
Now she turns her face from him and the cold
and thinks only of the present and of stone...

She thinks of building houses of stone,
and she thinks of smooth blocks of time.
And she wraps herself with plans from the cold
of how to escape the rattling sparrows.
Somehow her eyes have lost their color and the rainbow
vanished from her heart like tears in the wind.

She calls him her pine bough shaking in the wind.
She calls him her foundation, her limestone.
And still the name shivers in the cold. "rainbow.".
And he wonders if she has forgotten the time
when the wind seemed to stop and hold sparrows
from falling dead in the street, in the cold

And she never thinks about birds or cold,
except when the house rattles from the wind,
and noises fly above the house of stone,
and the cacophony of sparrows

flap their wings and forget time.
Then she searches the sky for a rainbow.

Neither he nor she has ever seen a rainbow.
They are both mostly timid and cold.
Then they remember the time
when they rattled and shook in the wind.
The foundation is laid for her house of stone,
and he pounds on the stone like the heart of a sparrow.

And she pounds on the stone like the beak of a sparrow.
And she calls her house a rainbow.
And her heart beats like a wing on the stone.
And she is no longer afraid of the cold.
or when she is caught up in the wind.
and she is thin in the large figure of time.

Both he and she no longer notice the cold.
They are building rainbows in the wind
And they make houses out of time.

My Hip Grandma

Who danced at my cousin's wedding, went
to Hong Kong, the Philippines, and made up stories
about everything. Whose husband came from
Russia and stole her from her Brooklyn family.
Who quit school early to go to the movies and listened
to my poetry. This is the grandma who, like a clock
that gets behind cannot catch up. She relives the
past, warns of the Red threat, and won't shut up.
She used to say, "I'm your hip grandma, I'll never
grow old." But she did like furniture you think is
dusty but has holes.

Toots we call her. Toots, the overbearing, lively
grandma who puffed at cigarettes and tucked us
into bed. Tough and stuffed and loving us too much,
she never let us go. We sneaked away, but her
words became our dreams. "Somewhere in a misty
mountain village, people live forever."

Stay Toots, stay. Already you slip away. Tell me
one more time about your revolutionary father who
wouldn't buy you shoes for school or your sister
Ray.... Old age does something to people you say
Keep dancing at Arthur Murray. Dance! Dance!
I'll find a way to make you young.

Sharing

We share this planet with the breeze,
the seasons, neon obliterating stars.
Months like broken promises.

We share this planet with the ocean
moon churning the tides.
Electrons and canyons.

We share this planet with each other
with thumbs who also forgive.
We begin and end with a flurry like snow
then melt and evaporate.

This planet of love and woe,
dust and blood,
we share with the bomb.
Only the sun sees all.

Soundlessly

This land of buildings, cone shaped, flat,
slanting, we inhabit like birds fill the forest.
We steal light from the stars, contaminate
our waters. Our sons and daughters grow up
with the irony we can rule an office, destroy
it all, and still children carry a lunch to school,
sleep soundlessly.

The Dream

In the morning early, I wish to speak to you.

I have so much to say. It is

a full moon. Darkness turns bluer. What

I want to say is like a prayer of a dream,

something soft spoken and unreal. And I must

save this until you have awakened. By then

the moon too has grown blue. I want to tell you

what this world is made of, that there is a bigger

world beyond us, beyond our comprehension. My

words fail me. I am speaking to no one. By light,

the birds have arisen, the paper boy slaps a paper

at the front door, and the trash man swings around

another turn on the empty streets.

Those Things I'm Most Afraid Of

Being lost in a blizzard
of dreams,
the insect, the moth
in my stomach,
being motherless, making lists..

Bats tangling in my hairs,
you reaching for my
hairs,
falling backwards,

Swallowing fish bones,
overdosing on wishes,
being dependent on a caress,
being sexless,
being sought after
by terrorists,

Falling into manholes
being committed
to the extinction of moths,

the smell of iodine, the smell
of you after you've left,
Being run over

by your hands,
Being transplanted, losing
an organ, internal bleeding,

Being drugged by a feather,
smothered by a whisper,
waking up an inmate
of myself, my most intimate
listener,

Snow shoeing through my
thoughts, hugging

a shadow, the crack
in my voice, having
no voice.

My Soul

My soul came cascading down
like a brief thunderstorm.
And the leaves shook
And all around me there was
fear, fear, fear.

My soul like a blind skydiver
landed in the ocean
in deep, deep waters.
And I hardly missed it.

Except when love entered the equation.
But even then my soul seemed
remote, indifferent, cold.

But it was still my soul.
So I followed it down my street.

How it got there I don't know,
but my soul seemed to know
So I followed it till we were both lost.

And it was then that my soul
became my best friend.
And they say when I die,
it will ascend to heaven.

The Nation's Capitol

The maze, glazed windows of Woodward and
Lothrop, sidewalks leading from Kennedy Center
Amazement down to 14th and New York where the
remnants of a burnt school building lie and hookers
smoke joints in the cool air at night. This is no
place for the casual tourist. It takes the experienced
eye of the voyeur, trained in his craft, down to the
last naked detail of her heel. No shoes, her hair
matted, she sleeps on the bench at the park at
17th and I street while I eat my lunch and wait to
see my dentist who charges by the candy-bar.

This is a city of changes. Like my young black
friend said recently, "If I don't get a job soon,
I'm going to start killing people." Watergate is a
landmark of one man's grandiose deception.
Condos collide with window shops in my old
neighborhood throwing out eighty-year-old
tenants. The city changes at night. It changes
in the day. At night it's dangerous all over but
it's beautiful even down on 14th street where cops
and rats fill the alleyways. Night somehow
makes the city silent, a haven for lovers, loud
bursts of rock and roll, families bunched together,

rapists, bicyclists, joggers, brave women riding
the subway home, the click of their heels.,
arguments heard from the street, and men pacing
the sidewalks.

By day the city moves, it flashes, it yawns.
Buses pull out of their stations, and with a jolt
everyone is transformed with coffee and their
first cigarette.

I wanted to show you this city. Down from the
dirty Potomac to the fish market. I wanted you
to love this city or to love me or both. It isn't
easy seeing a 14-year-old boy picked up in a
Cadillac at 4 AM. It isn't easy to know that you
can't love me or even try. I thought we could ride
through this city out to Virginia and back down to
Anacostia. I'm not losing you am I? If you can't

believe in what that black woman was screaming
at her son, " Go on boy, this is *your* city as well
as *theirs*!" then you can't ever believe me.
Misery is a part of the ecology of this city. It is
haunted by wealth and overshadowed by everyone
else. If you can't know this city then there must
be something seriously lacking in our relationship.
If you can miss that traffic light so easily then

we are headed for a collision. If you can't stop
and look at the drivel, filth, chuckle, jerk,
screech, odor, slop, brush, scream, pain,
then babe, I believe we were not meant
for each other.

Why I Gave Up and Wrote a Computer Poem

My computer has a virus.
The printer isn't working.
Neither is the CD player,.
It's twenty degrees outside.
I'm fending off cabin fever.

What did our forefathers do on a long Friday?
They couldn't fill up the hours without Google, Facebook and
Twitter.
Did they discuss Indian raids not Osama Bin Laden?

I can't fill up the hours
without Google, Facebook or Twitter.
My computer has a virus.
It's too cold for a walk in the garden.

I read the news online-
Keep up with friends on email.
What can I do without a CD player,
printer and computer?

I've read all the books in my condo.
It's too cold to walk to the library.
If it snows, I'll have to find someone
with whom to cuddle.

I'll have to find someone with whom
to cuddle. My computer has a virus.
It's mid-December,
I actually haven't met you yet——
I'm waiting to meet you on the computer.

Counting

My Zen Master taught us to stare at a wall,
and recite from one hundred backward
and then forward and so on...

When I wait for the metro,
I meditate,
I also count how many hours I sleep,
how many calories I eat,
how many miles to my destination.

Numbers juggle themselves—
add, subtract, deduce
and arrive out of nowhere like a square foot.

An isosceles triangle follows me down the street.
The unknown quantity x appears in my dreams.
A tangent or cotangent plots my waking hours
I sum up the inventory of my cluttered mind.

In the end, I will hold my breath and count to infinity
and backwards,
without uttering a number.

Anxiety

Like a grinning chimp
I am nervous as snow
scattering, shimmering, freezing.

I wake with a crow in my throat.
Nightmares dance around my apprehension.
A blue, blue sky turns me into a statue.

I think, I fear.
Behind my smirk, I am petrified
of being alone, an old hurt.

When I come closest to being alive
I panic like a marlin caught in a net
and thrown back.

And terrified of death,
not only my own,
but the sun, someone I love…

My anxiety keeps reoccurring
like the theme of a symphony.
And the attacks grow stronger
like a crescendo.

Until they are resolved by the moon,

who takes my fears and

turns them into a shining.

Renovation

The cabinets demand,
"Don't dismantle us."

The carpets shudder
as we tear them up.
The walls have tribulations
we console with paint.

The furniture complains
about being pushed around.

We cover holes
with plaster earplugs

The windows and doors open
to their discontent.

We must give the condo a time out
while it recovers
from these amputations.

Where am I?

My mother wants to know
why she can't remember.
A brain tumor, I say, they removed
a brain tumor from your head.
Then she wants to know where is she?
How did she get here?

And I am here to assist
Since I don't have a job
And it is January-a year since
her first surgery.

And I learned the word metastasized
when we almost lost her.

My mother is our sun.
She is with us a day or a lifetime
She will leave us in darkness.

Where am I? she asks,
You're here, mom, we're with you
you're home.

Broken Wing

My friend has a broken wing
that never heals.

Like a pigeon she pecks at
crumbs from passersby.

She is happy to be cooing songs
every morning for me.
She is happy just to be
to be a bird that cannot fly.

Something like a pelican on one foot,
she has one good wing
that flaps about in the wind.

And then she is taken back into the sky
in her song
but only in her song.

Diary of Psychiatric Mediations Taken by Patient MS

Thorazine—Initially used in first hospitalization.
Totally wiped me out.

Librium —Prescribed by Dr. M. for separation anxiety.
Got manic. Insanely in love with male dancer.

Lithium—Prescribed by Dr. M. for manic/depression.
Caused physical pain in the chest, and didn't keep me
from getting manic.

Stellazine—Prescribed by Dr. M. for psychosis.
(caused me to be legally blind when I used it later with Dr. D.)
I also OD'd on it. I thought strangers were famous people.
I was the color purple orange, I was gay. I was the messiah.
.

Mellaril—Liked the "mellow" effect became my psychotic drug
of choice. (later under Dr. E. caused holes in my eyes)

Haldol—Hated. Cut me off from my feelings but quickly snapped
me out of mania.

Tegretal— NIH experimental double blind program. In seclusion
for two weeks —danced inside the walls, prayed to Allah. Then with
Dr. W.—it kept me out of the hospital. Seemed to work. Got Master's
Degree.

Tegretal and Mellaril— Dr R. I broke through medication.
Hospitalized.

Dr. D. put me on everything—
Prolixin-hyped me up and exhausted me, caused pacing
Resperidon—got me angry and irritable Tegretal.
Halcion —I believe I had a terrible reaction to it-
lack of control of muscles or that could have
been from the mixture of so many meds that Dr. D.
used at once including Stellazine (made me legally blind).
I would get anxiety attacks every day at work. Add to that
my addiction to liquor and you can imagine the side effects.
Inability to keep me from getting manic.

Threw all my meds down the toilet.
Ended up at GW, then Sibley.
I think was maintained on Mellaril and Tegretal.
Called the weather and spoke to an imaginary friend.
The rings answered me.

Saw Dr. E.

Had to get off the Mellaril because it caused holes in my eyes.

Put me on Klonopin. Had to keep taking more to get same effect.

Or I was drunk on it. OD'd on Klonopin. Went into GW

Hospital—put me on Dr..P.'s suggestion—Depakote and Clozapine.

Worked for fifteen years. Got rid of the delusions. Towards the

end of seeing Dr. E. got on Neurotin, and switched Lamicatal for

Depakote because of my hand tremor.

Stayed on Clozapine.

Seroquel— Dr. G. Initially put me on but wiped me out.

Falling and dizzy— lost job at UDC.

Neurontin— Didn't work well-still suffered from anxiety attacks

regularly. But the sedation made it a seductive drug. It caused me

incontinence,

falling, fatigue.

Continued with Lamicatal.

Clozapine.

Then change to

Buspar—I don't know what it does

Atavan, temporary and very little relief from anxiety

Abilify—makes me nauseous, not sure what it does.

Clozapine

That's all I remember

Small Miracles

I was high and ended up late at night
roaming the streets with only prostitutes for company.
Or when I almost died in Brooklyn, when I got
off at the wrong stop—with no money, drunk, someone gave
me the change for a bus back.

Funny, how I think God is with me, the footprints
in the sand, God carrying me. When it's only my
crazy sense of direction and my tenacity to live
that got me through the rape and West, the prostitute, walking me
home.
I thought I would walk forever. In the morning, they put me in PI,
drugged me and put me in restraints.

Now reality shines through behind a cloud.,
the sun at dusk. The sun doesn't revolve around me.
I can look but not too long or it will hurt my eyes
Sometimes, being with you hurts. But it is nothing
compared to losing my mind.

A Woman I Met at Sibley Hospital

Mother, Father

I want my mother and my father.

I saw my father beaten by the Nazis.

Where are my keys?

Somebody help me find my car key.

She is my daughter.

How can 1 turn my back on her?

I can't find it

I can't find anything.

Let there be peace.

That's all I want.

Why can't we just be a family?

1 don't know where 1 put it.

Where is- my car key?

If only we could just get along.

That's all I ask God.

I just want my mother and my father.

Where are they?

Somebody help me; I can't find my car key.

There is only one man I will ever love.

He died.

Why am I crying?

1 can't find anything.

I want my mother and father.

She is my daughter.

How can 1 turn my back on her?

I can't find it

I can't find anything.

Let there be peace.

That's all I want.

Why can't we just be a family?

Red Eye Car Trip to New York

Where did we begin to fight?
We took a trip to New York.
a red eye car trip. I slept in the back seat while
your brother drove. By 2AM we were at loose ends.

We stayed with your friends, relatives. It was a eulogy for a woman I
didn't know. Your brother cried. I was in a room of strangers.
The Oneg Shabbat was good, a bagel and lox and some egg salad.
I was hungry and tired.

On the way back I was afraid you were going to cheat me the way my
father warned me men would.

I was furious. You were livid. I refused to pay my share that night
at dinner with your relatives. You screamed at me. It was as if a
tsunami hit me *I was so sure I was right.* You said I was acting like a
JAP. I don't know how we made up.

I was sure we almost lost each other.

Anniversary

This is the anniversary of your death.
When the chrysanthemums bloom,
I pick one from the garden. Spring is a time of renewal,
my birthday and the anniversary of your death.

I'd have done it differently. You kept asking does he love me?
Do I love him? And I wanted to promise you it was forever.
Everything dies. You never told me that.

There is the promise of summer in the air. Magnolias
blossom. Cherry trees. An awkward truth, sometimes it gets
so hot I can barely breathe. You stopped breathing.

The cicadas will be back this year. You return
in my dreams. I could have done it differently.
Loved you more, him less. .

Holding Back

Heat lightening—
the many colors of passion.
Mute first love.
Braiding pine needles,
listening to God in the forest,
Kumbaya by the campfire.

Man on the moon that summer.
I was fourteen.
Enamored, timid, holding back,
everything seemed possible.
And then the end of summer–
holding on to her like fruit clinging to the vine.

Now decades later,
remembering a child
who grew up like a cactus
holding her fervor inside a tough exterior.
Who later held on
like death to her companion.

And now the heavens flash
and I yearn. The leaves rustle with infatuation.
It is the summer solstice.

Dream State

Dreams abscond with me like
kidnappers holding me ransom
overnight.
They are the culprit behind
my out of control car,
the unrecognizable friends
that appear familiar
but foreign, the steep fall
I always wake up from.
Nightmares are fugitives of nonfiction,
the autobiography of the brain printed
as if in Braille. They are the beginning
and the end of a long tale.

They are a Pandora's box,
a whole can of worms, an
uncut version of a too long film
1 grope through them
with my imaginary cane—
They are the spook house.
They are the whore house.
They are the place for the criminally insane.

.

Tundra

Evergreens wrap their fingers
around me. Lichens suck and nudge and within
this crevice I'm cramped as a toad.
I'm so cramped I can barely breathe. I want
to unleash the rock and become one
with the tundra... I want
to be warm, moss-like and wind felt.

Is this a withering dream?
Morning is so cold and I'm numb
and alone and I move with the spirit
of a dream, and the brooks in my ears, the brook
in my ears...

The wind whirls through my thighs. It
teases me. Pain is smaller than a ripple.
And something lasts longer.

The sun's rays injure me. They brand
my petals. They soften the pollen in my breasts.
They singe my roots. Their searchlights
are endless.

The sun has its own ways. And the laws
I live by—the fraught brook,

the intoxicated mosquito, the lunatic
shadow. These things the wind and I delight in.
All day I imagine the color
of the wind's eyes.

Stark Morning Star

The silk grasses, the trees.....
All those things, we'd have done.

Stretched our eyes,
(abandoning each other)
pulled inward

or is that the way it's supposed
to be?

Near closing, every night
by clouds and clouds.
"Is that all right?"

I mean, I hear you move.

Acknowledgements

Barefoot Review	Faces on a Totem Pole
Chiron Review	Lenses
Emerge Literary Journal	Diary of Psychiatric Medications Taken by Intima Press Patient MS
Federal Poets Magazine	The Violin and the Lady in Black, What is Real, The Potomac is Still, Anniversary
Jewish Women's Literary Annual	Where Am I? A Woman I Met at Sibley Hospital
Hamby Stern Publishing	Jaylen
Little Magazine	Coals
Melusine	Faces on a Totem Pole, Totem Poles for Noah
Mary Mark Press	Renovation
Modern Images	Leather, The Cricket, The River, The Café, My Hip Grandma, The Nation's Capitol
Microw Review	Totem Poles for Noah, Small Miracles
The Flexist	Those Things I'm Most Afraid Of, Counting, Stark Morning Star
XLIbris	Augury, Tundra, Awakening, Dream State

Marjorie Sadin was born May 9, 1954, she has published poetry
nationally including in *The Emerge Literary Journal*, *The Barefoot
Review*, *Microw* and the *Jewish Women's Literary Annual*. She has four
books of poetry in print. Marjorie currently lives in the Washington
DC area and reads her poems locally. She is a docent
at the Library of Congress